AUGUST REVERIE IV
FANTASY ART ADULT COLORING BOOK

ISBN-13: 9798705942350

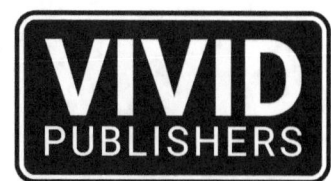

INTRODUCTION

Thank you for purchasing our adult coloring book August Reverie 4. You will find here twenty four intricate line art drawings for your coloring pleasure.

All art is hand drawn & line art shading is included as a guide to add shadowing & lighting.

You can use any coloring medium from pencils to markers as long as they have a fine tip.

A note on the use of markers: Even though the illustrations are printed one per page, to give additional protection please place a thick paper or cardboard beneath the page you are coloring so that the ink will not bleed through to the next page.

Subscribe at our website to get a FREE PDF Sampler featuring pages from our other adult coloring book releases! *Plus, news on discounts, free pages, contests and more!*

 *www.vividpublishers.com*

We would love to see your completed art. You can reach us at:

 *fb.com/VividPublishers*

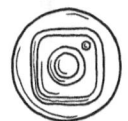 *@VividPublishers*

Also, we welcome you to join our Facebook group to share your art, see other colorists' art, enter exciting contests plus more!

 *fb.com/groups/VividPublishers*

Thank you for your continued support and interest in our adult coloring books. We hope you enjoy coloring the pages as much as we did creating them. Happy Coloring!

CONTENTS

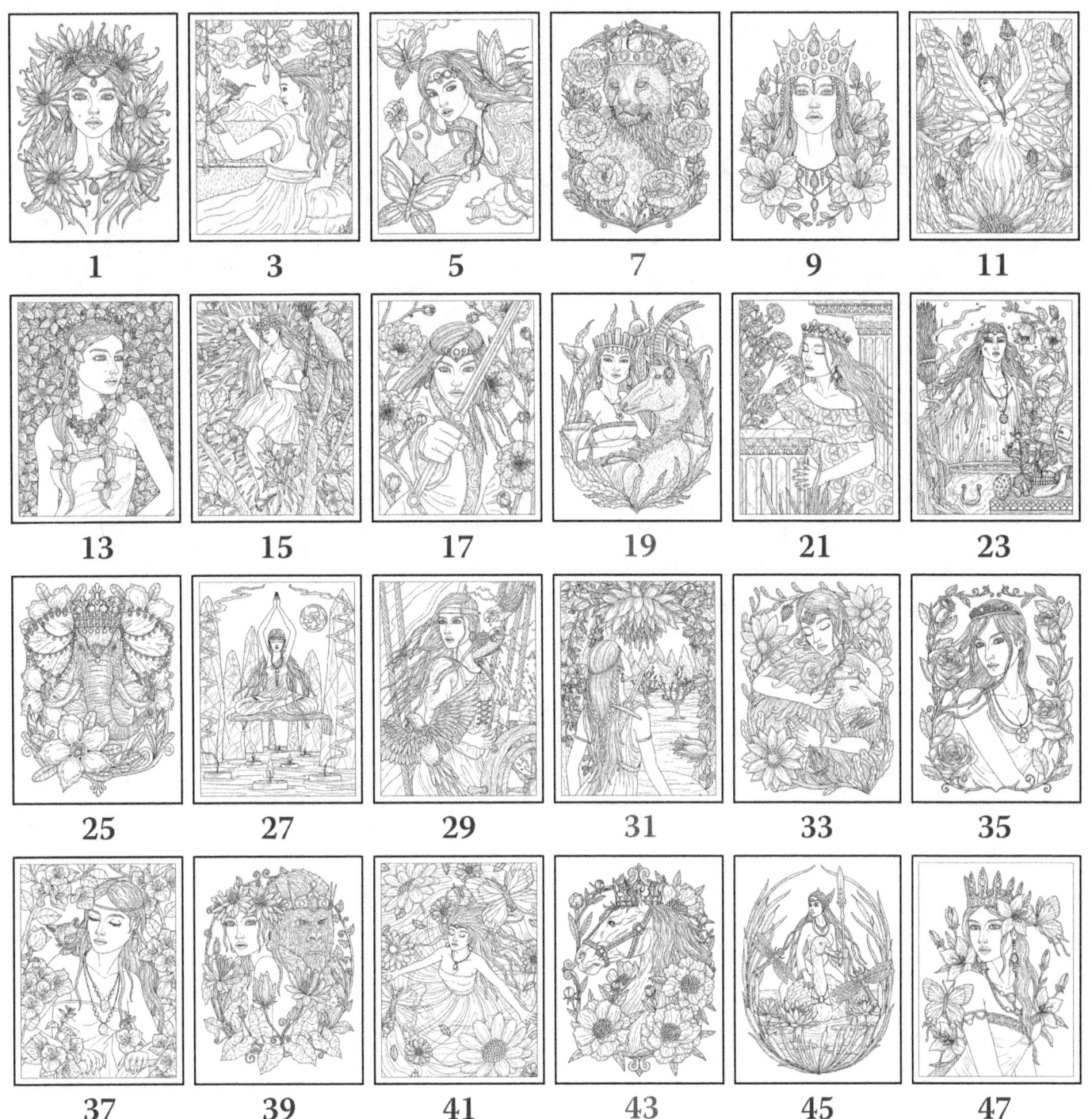

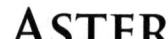

ASTER

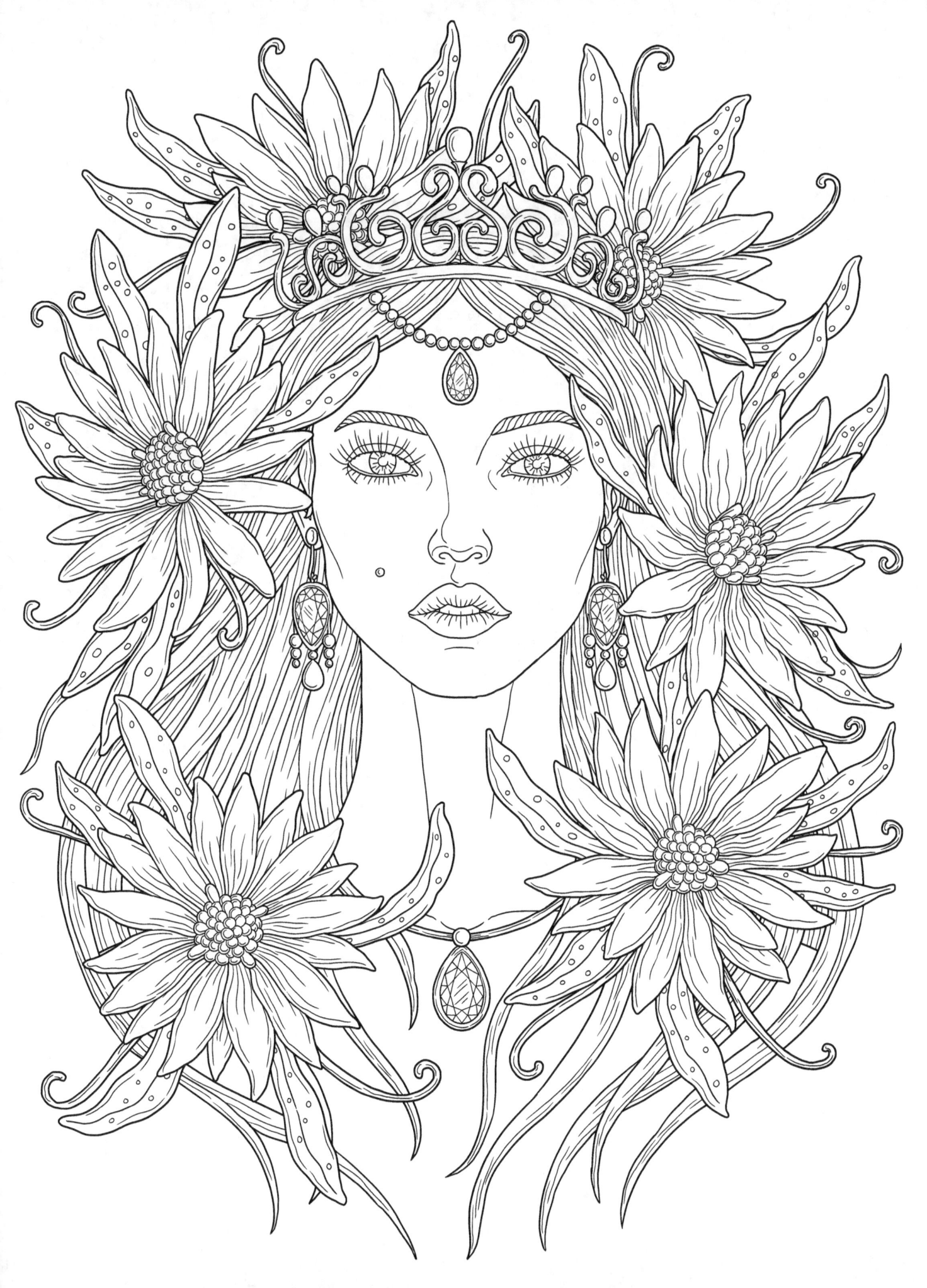

BIRD WHISPERER

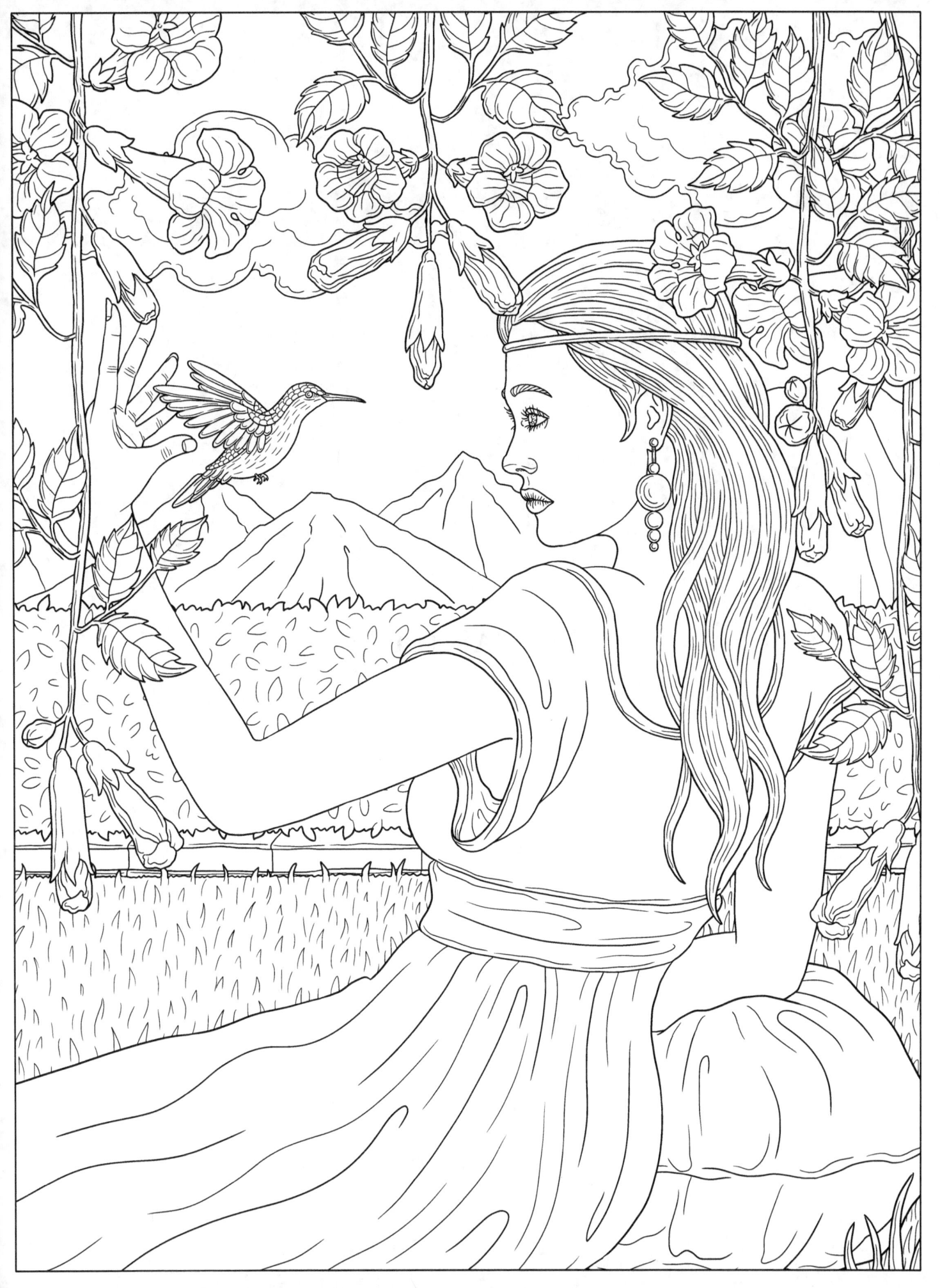

FLORAL THIEF

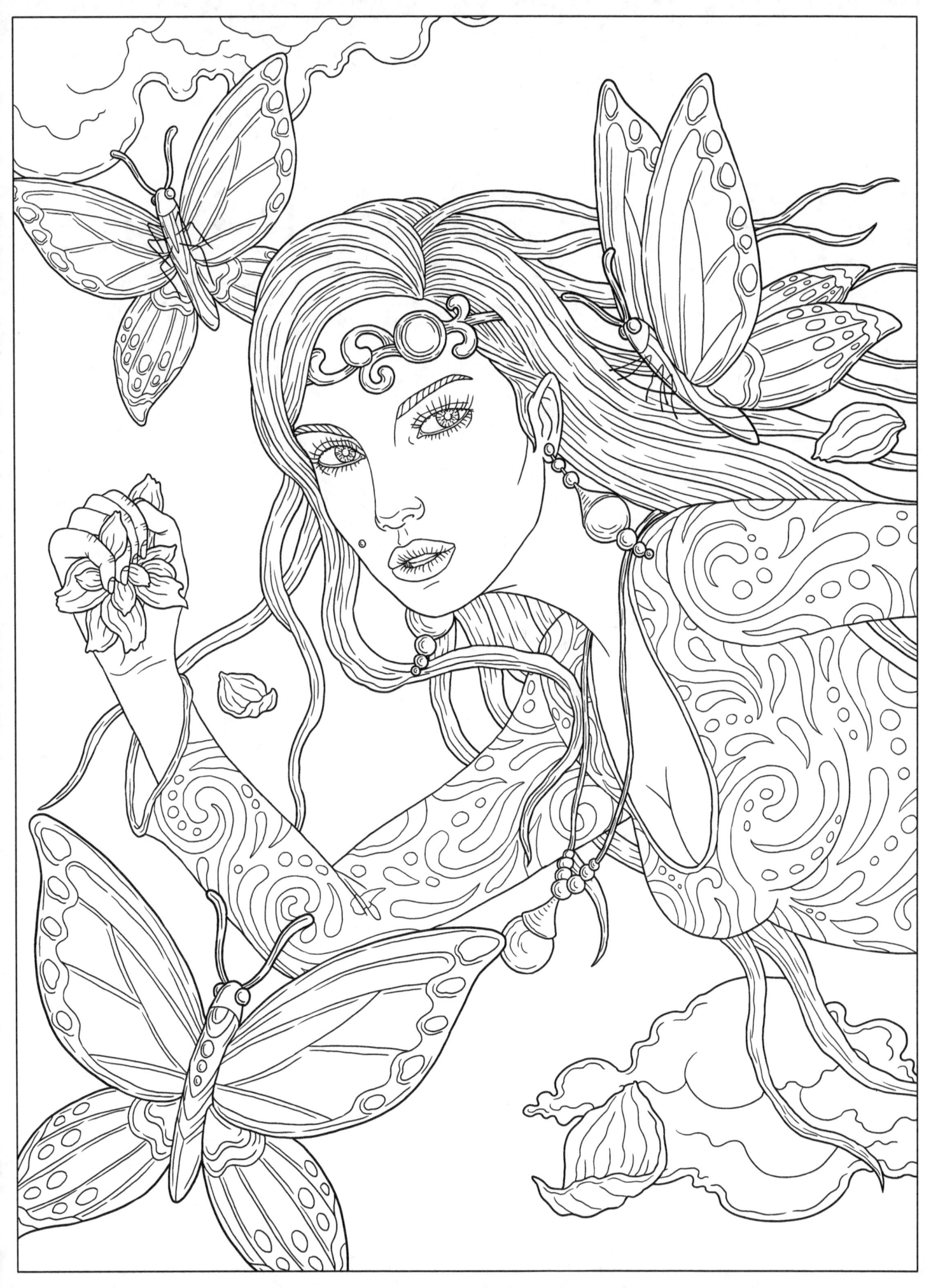

CHEETAH MAJESTIC

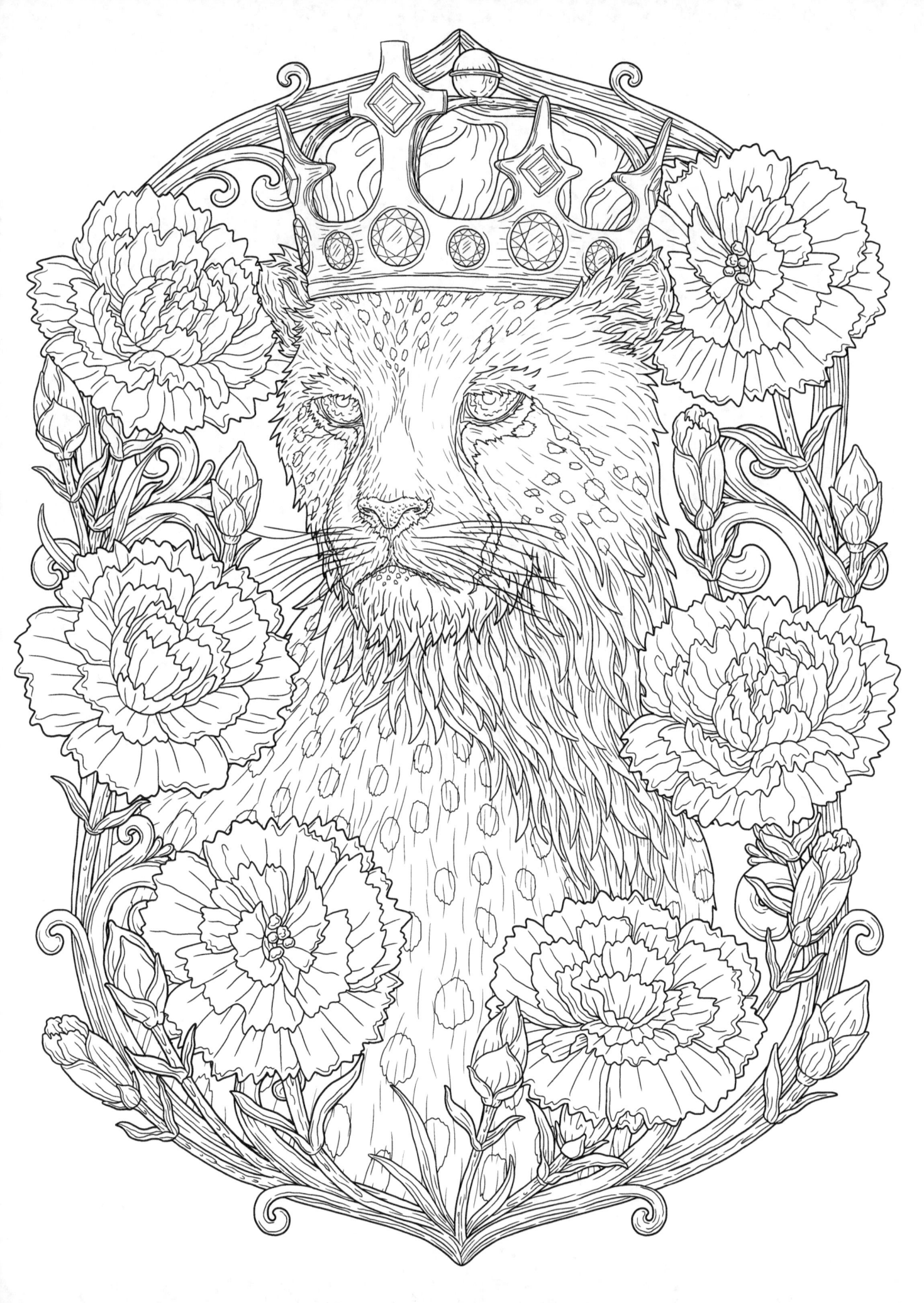

QUEEN AZALEA

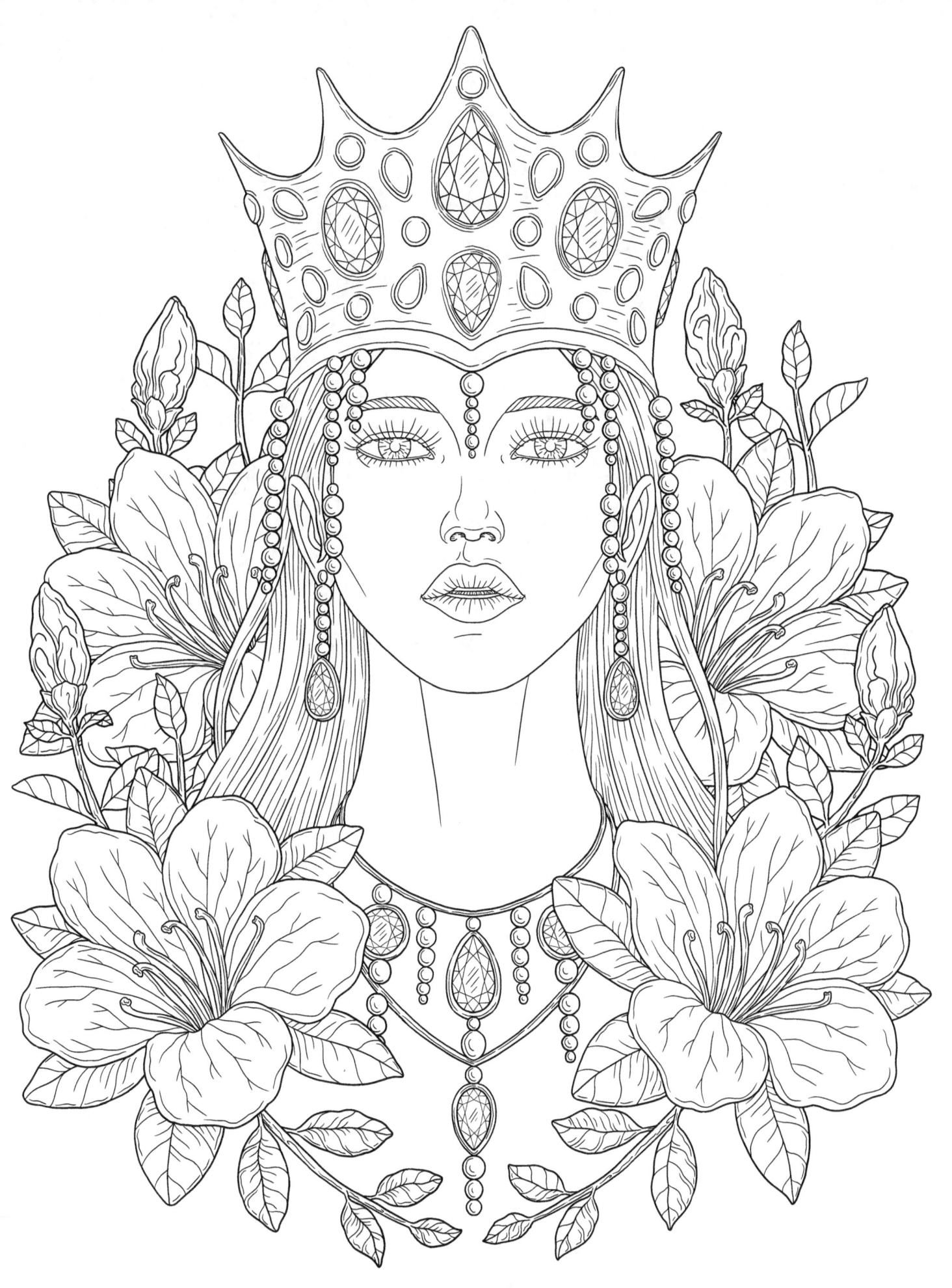

METAMORPHOSIS 2

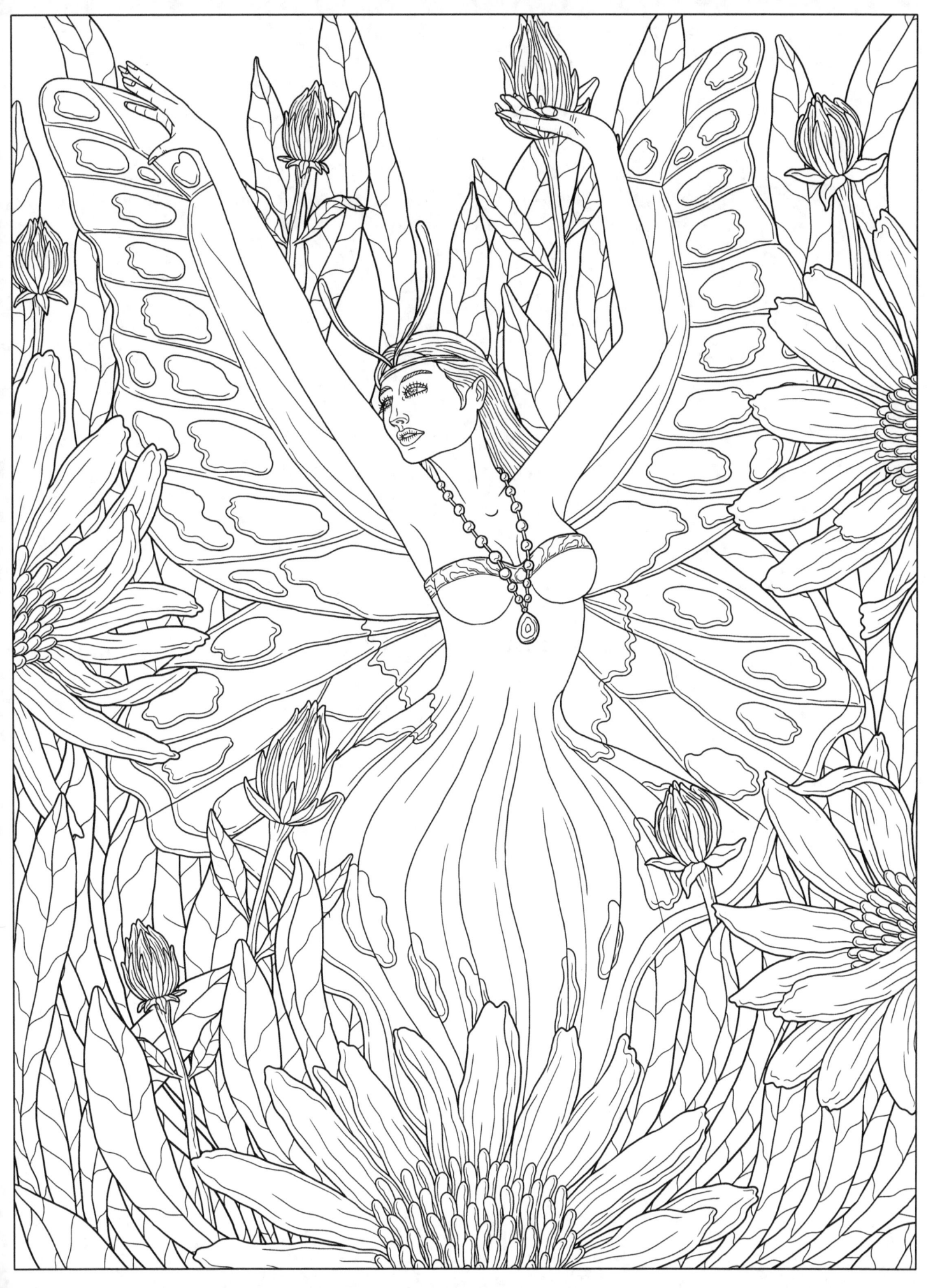

BELLFLOWERESS

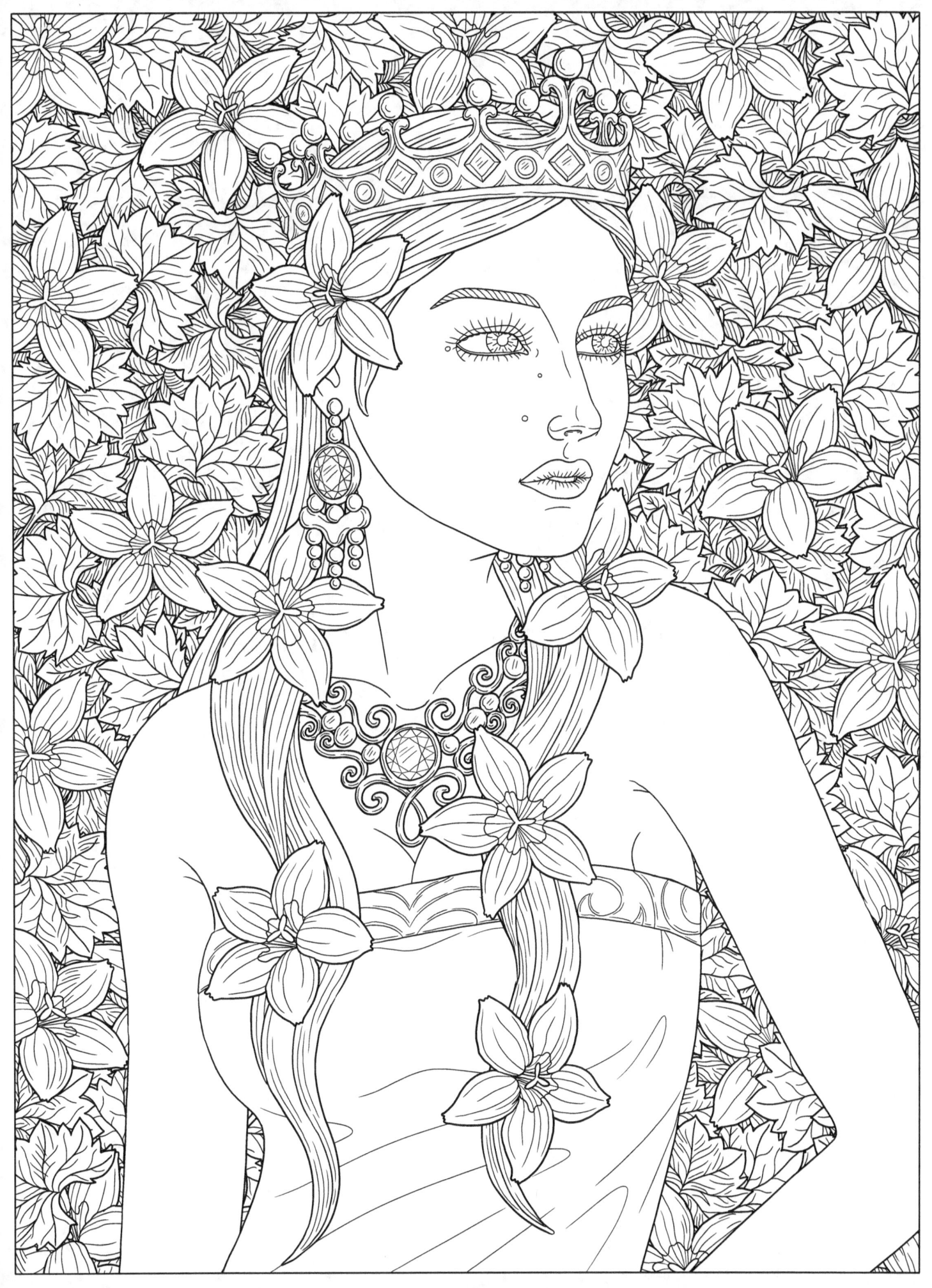

CALIFORNIA DREAMING

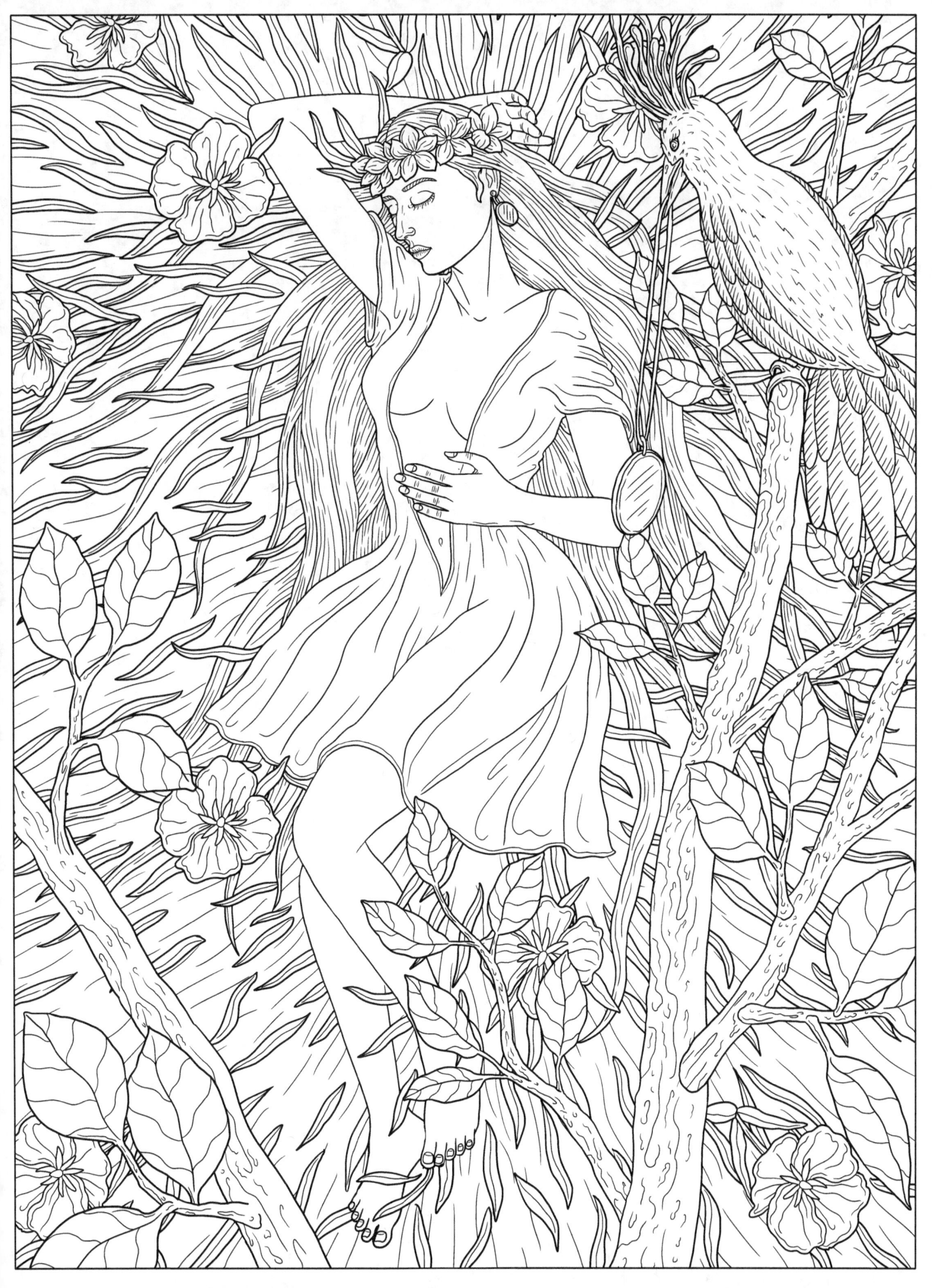

Armorer

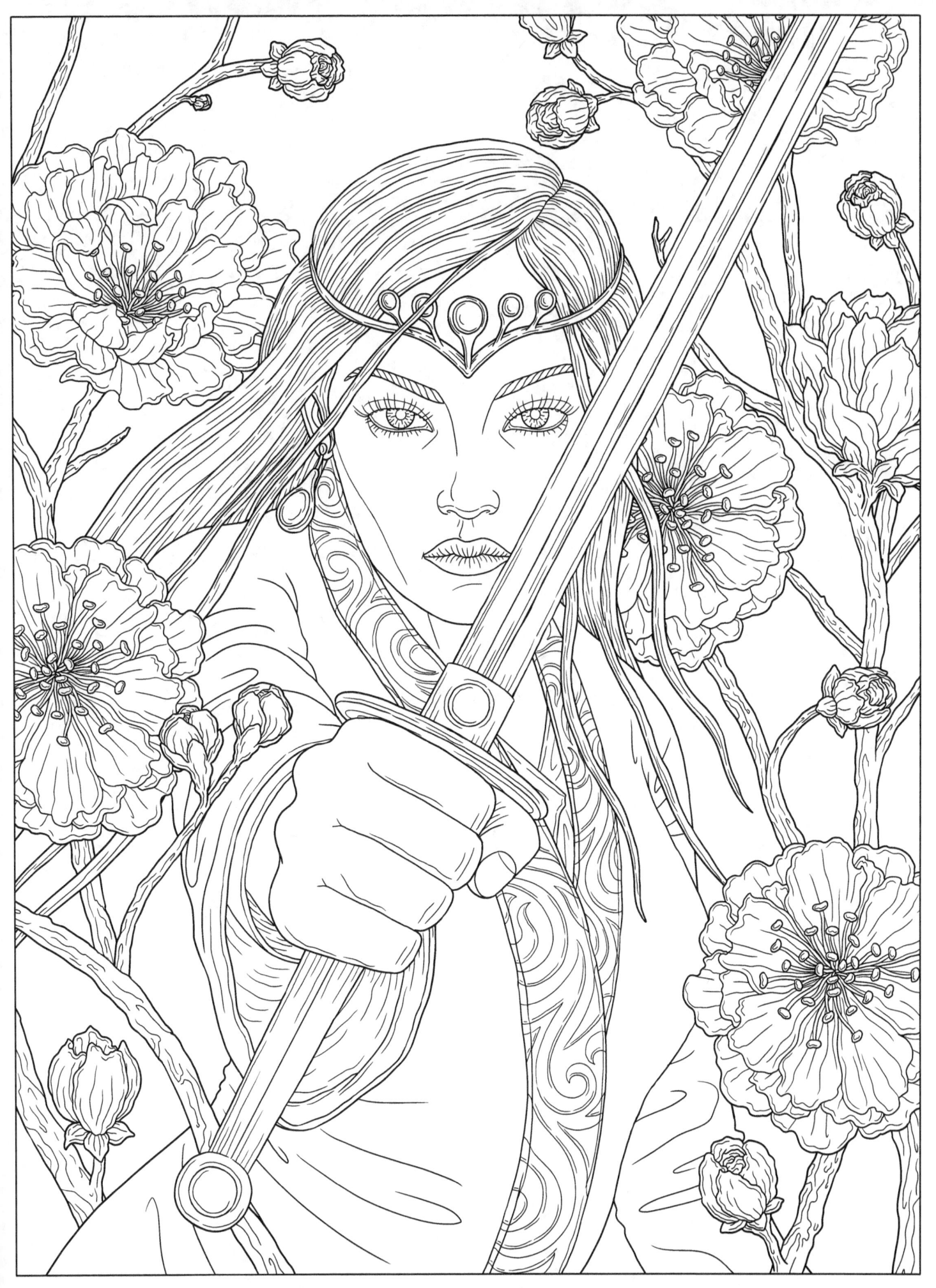

QUEEN SABLE

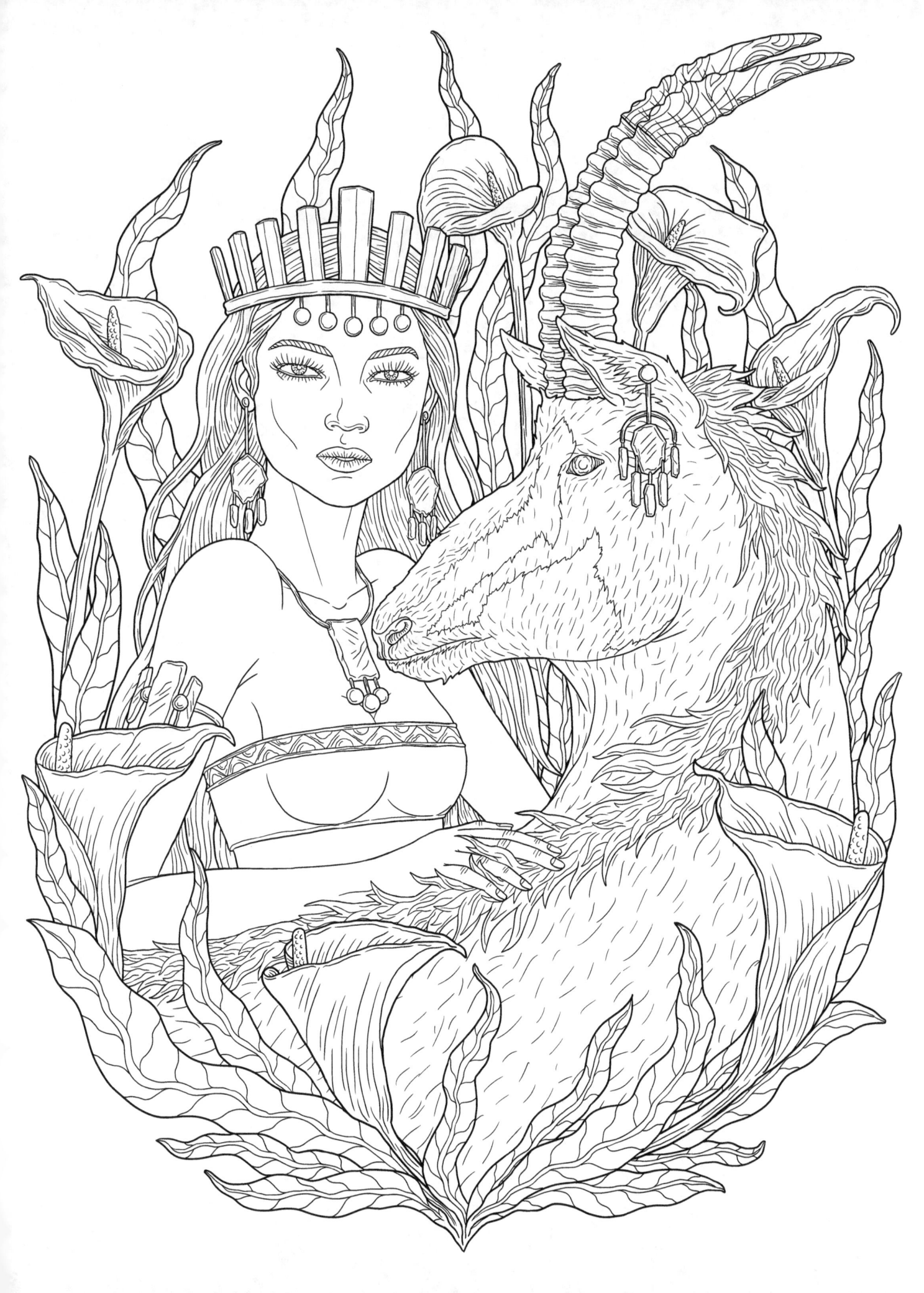

REACH OF FRAGRANCE

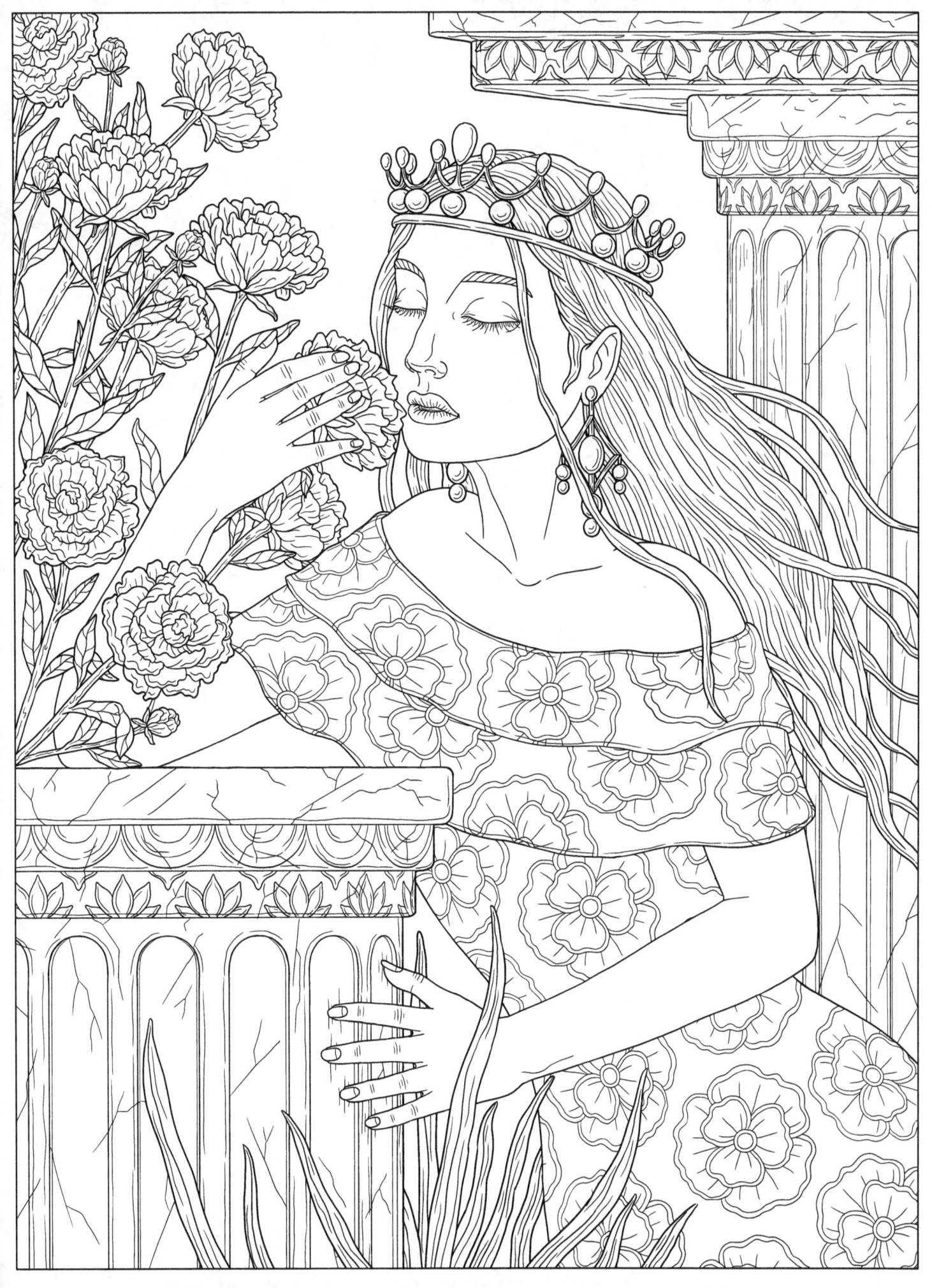

HALLOWEEN

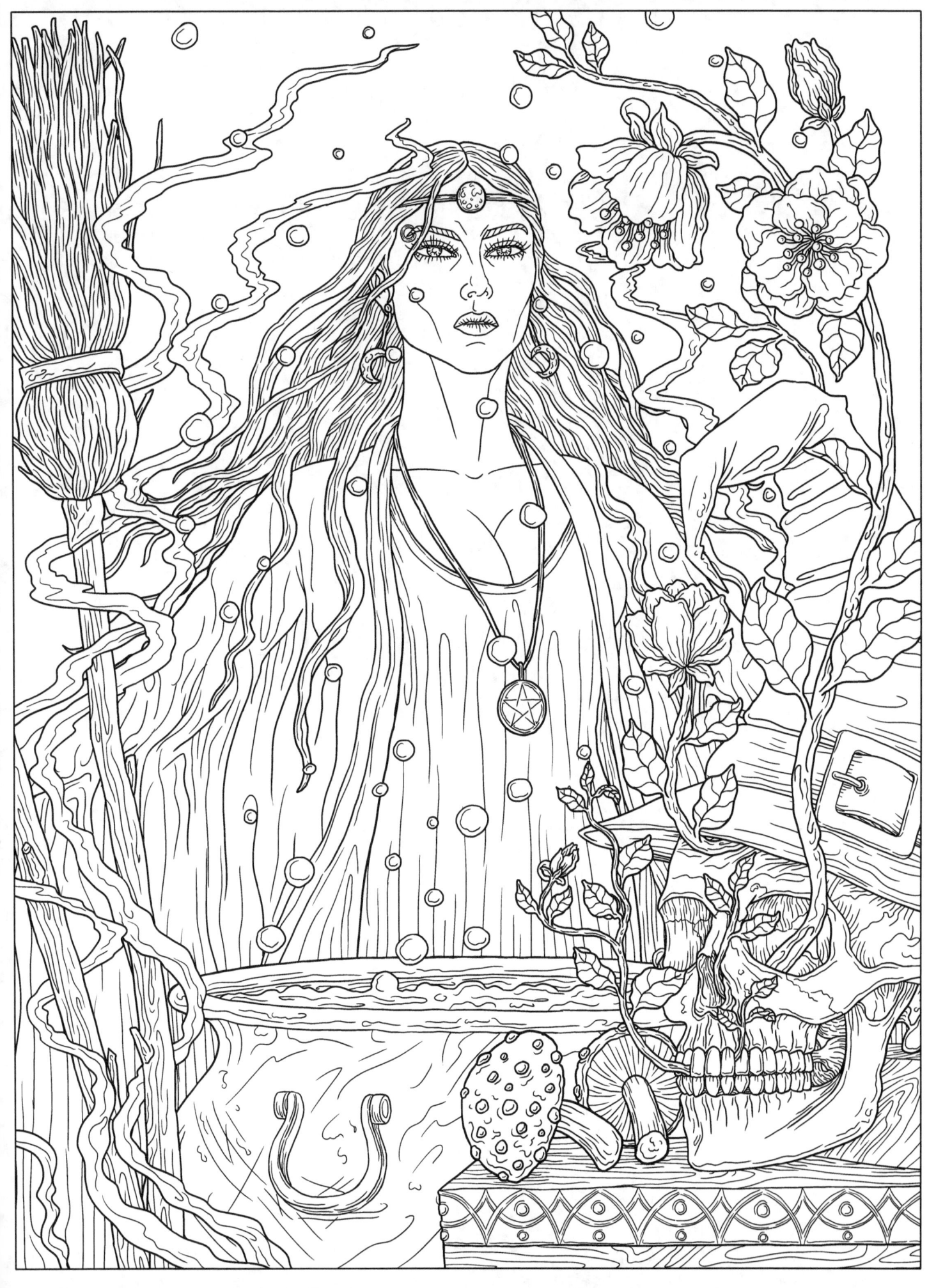

ELEPHANT MAJESTIC

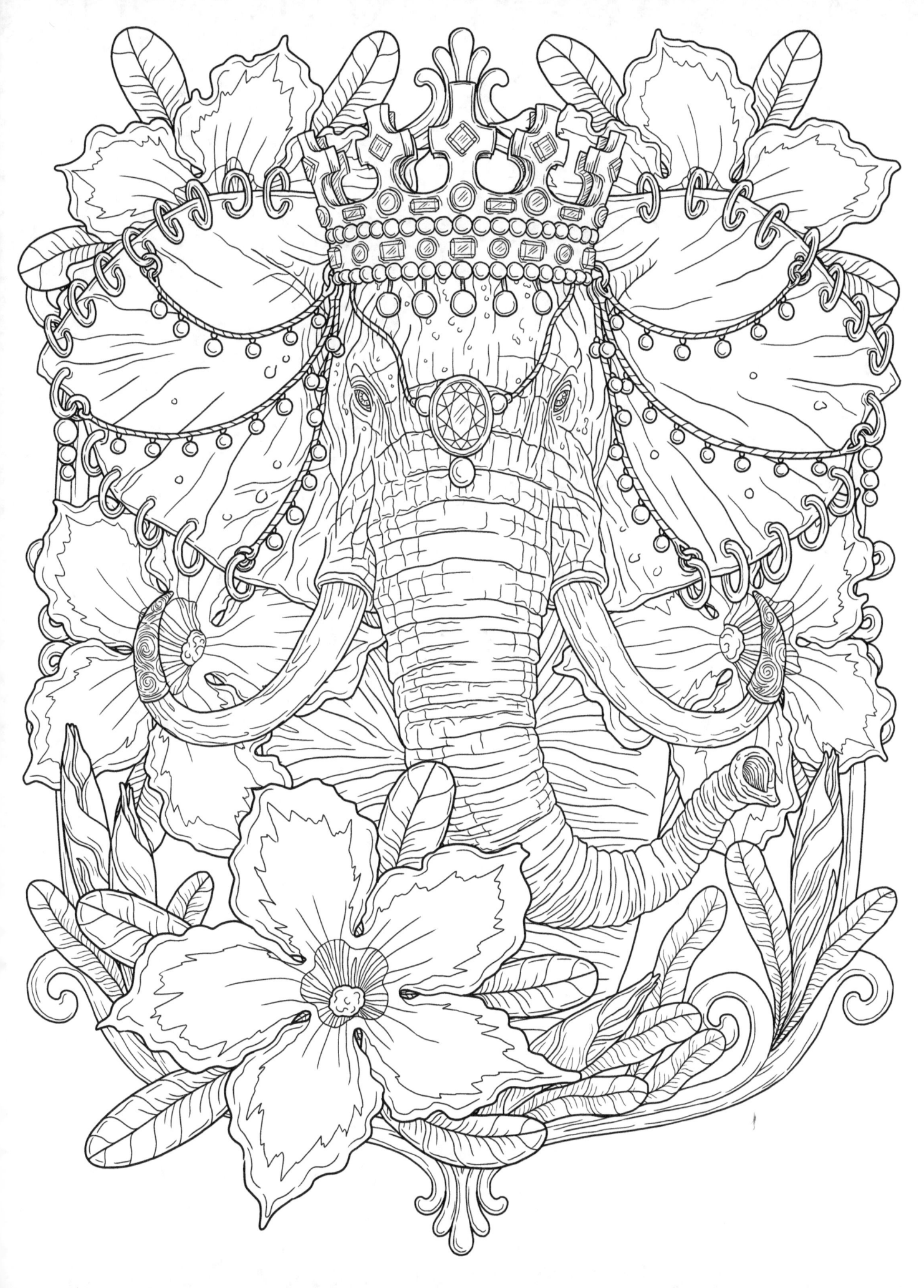

QUARTZ ROCK RISE

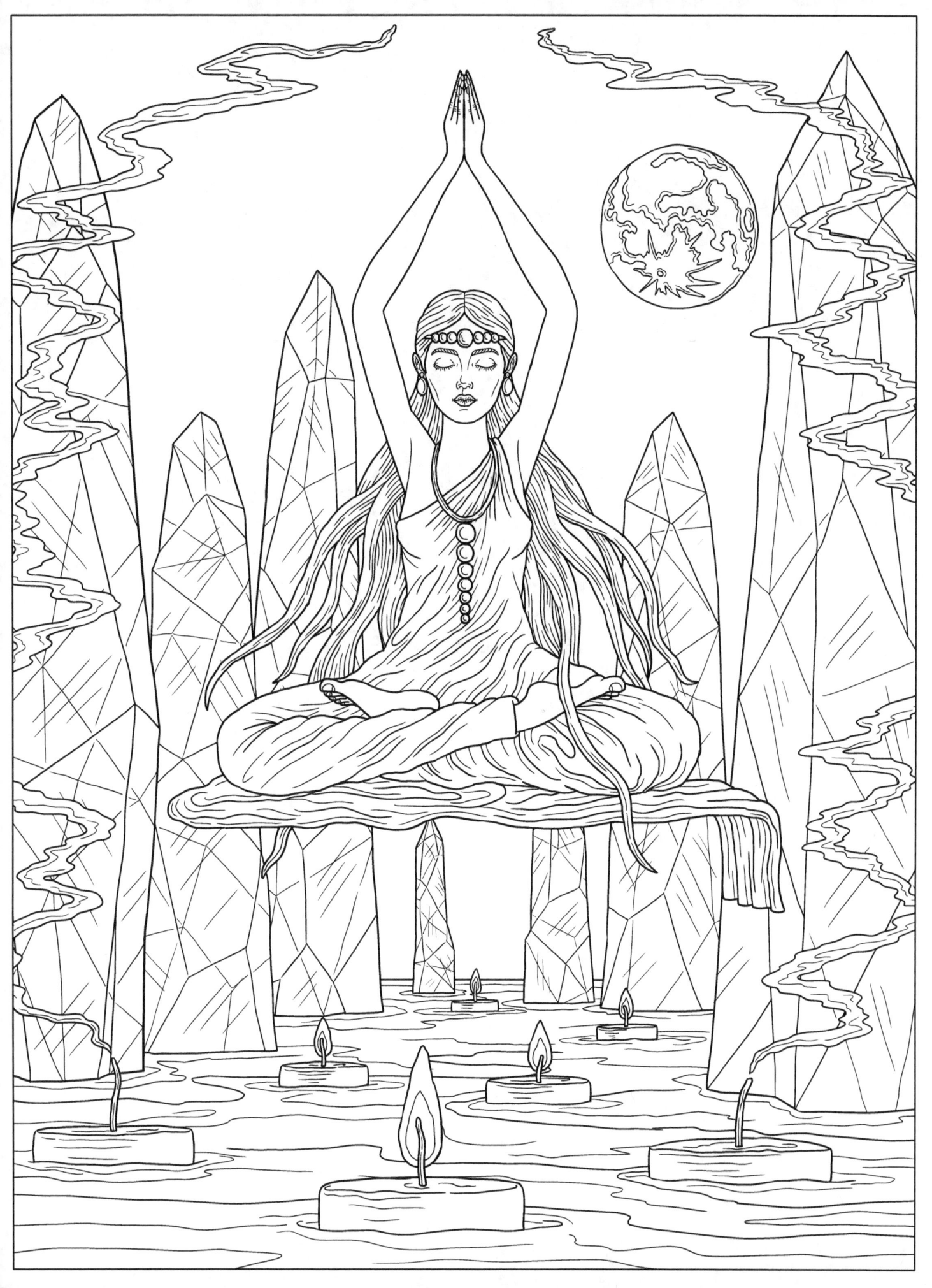

STORMY SEAS

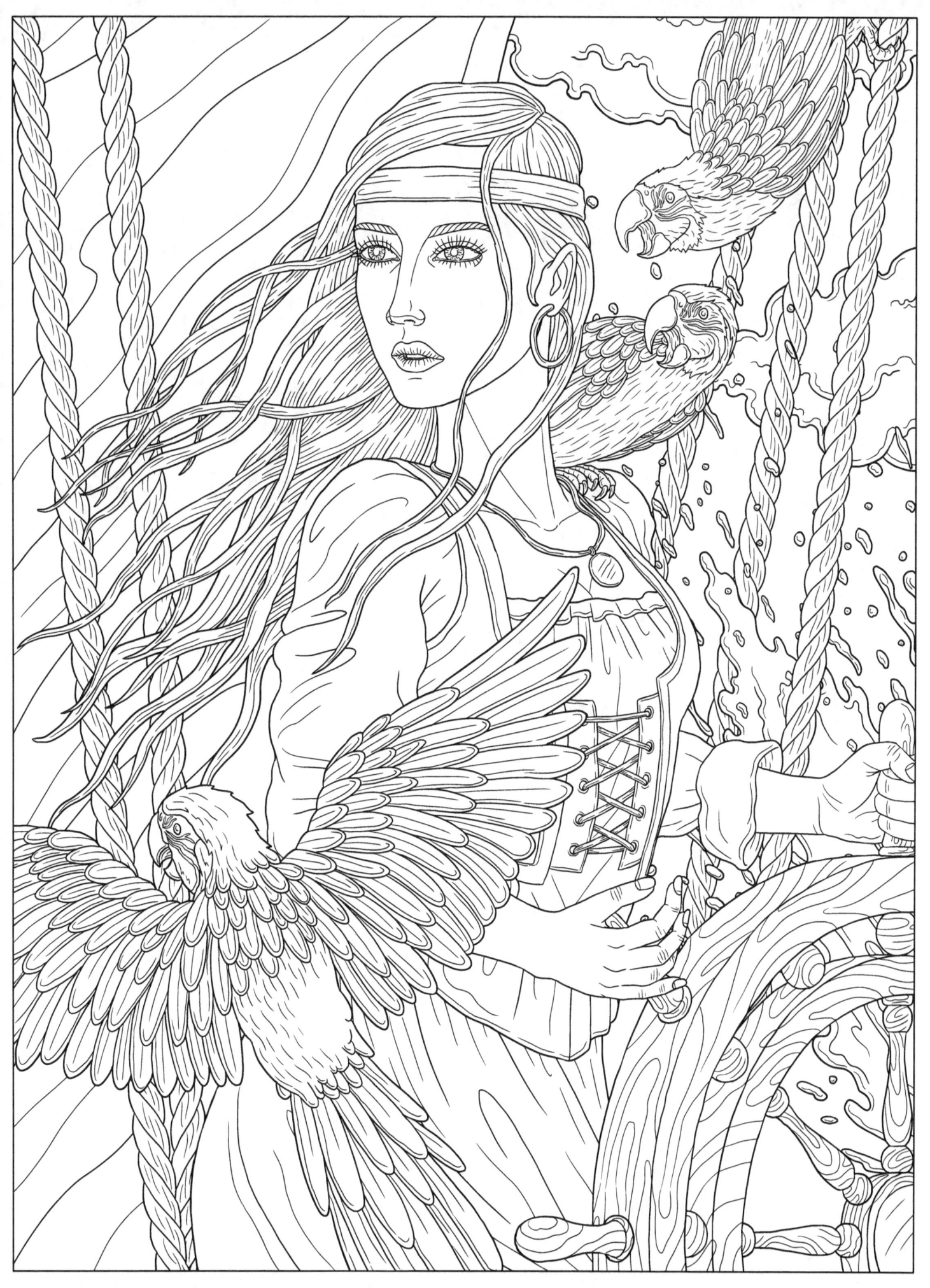

UNEXPECTED

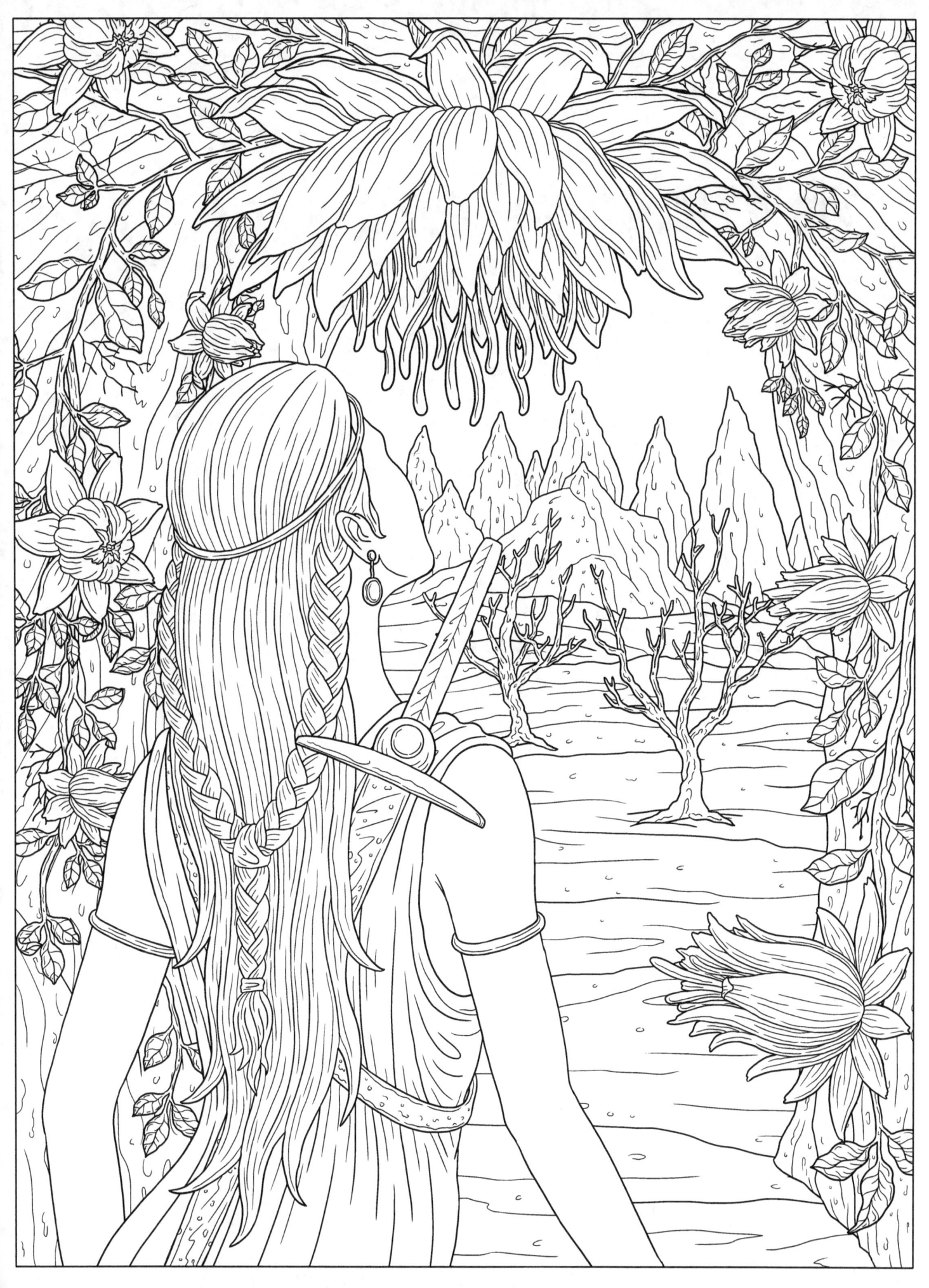

PANTHERA LOVE

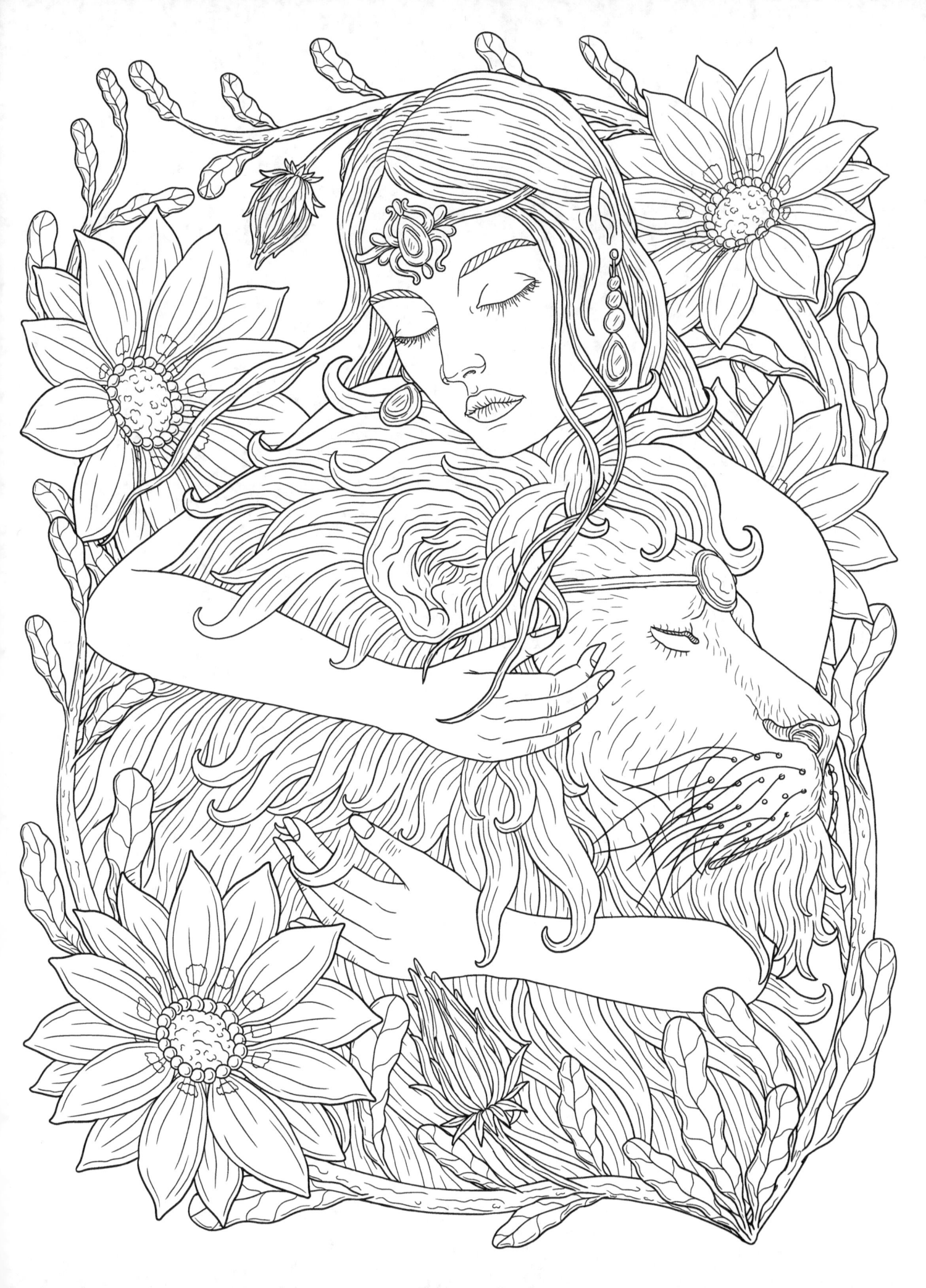

BELLEZA ROSE

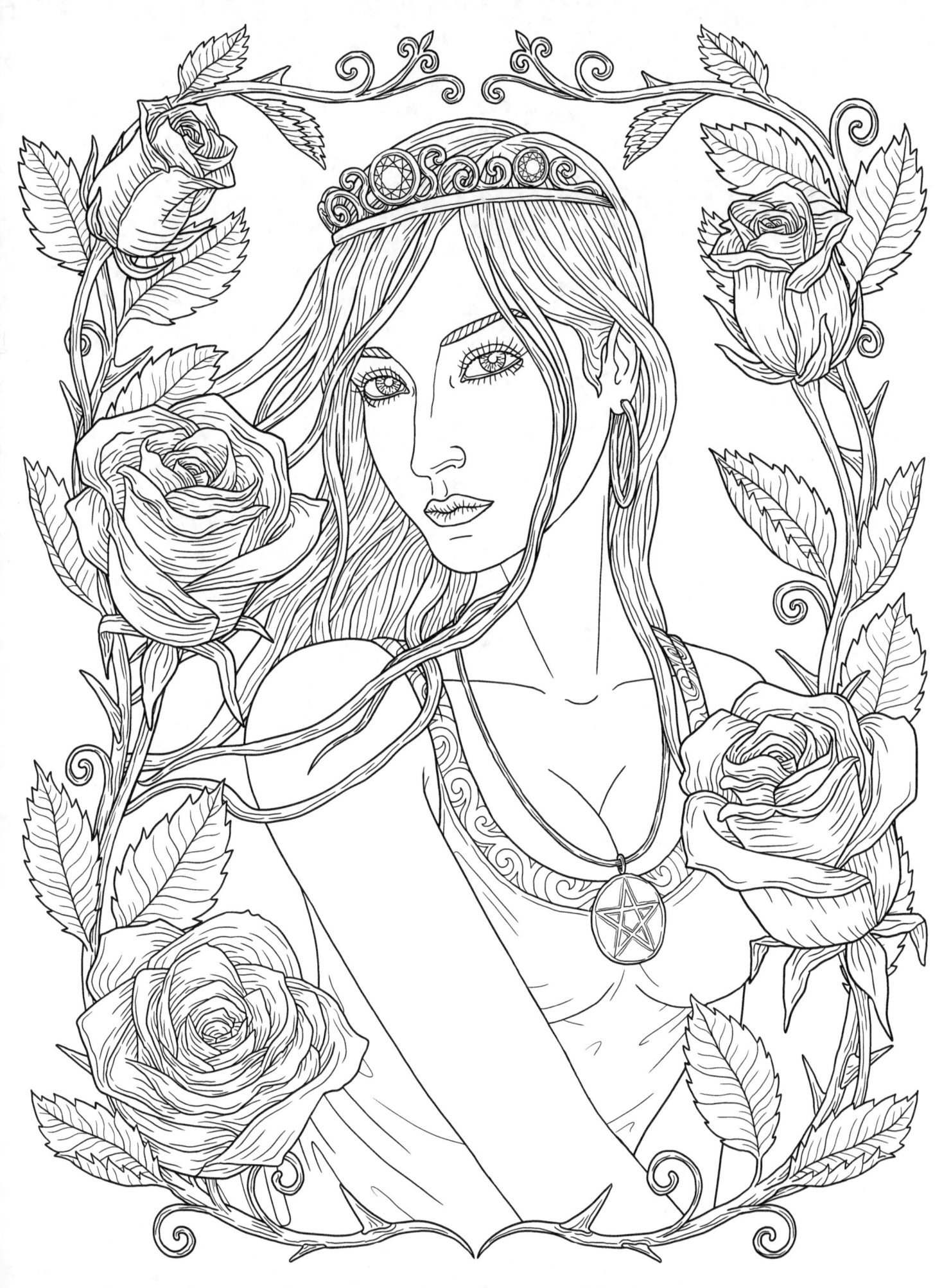

FELIDAE LOVER

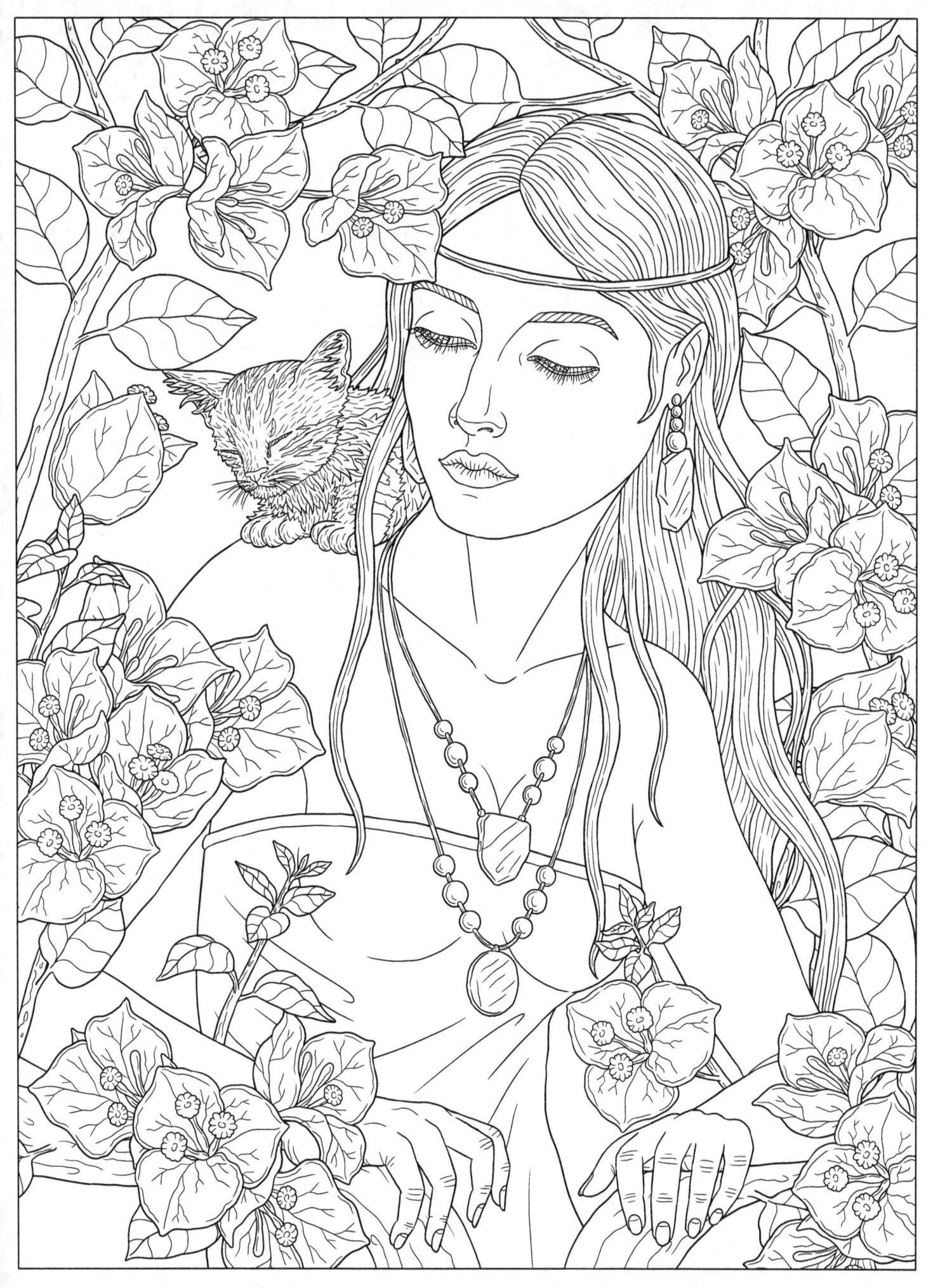

Beauty & the Silverback

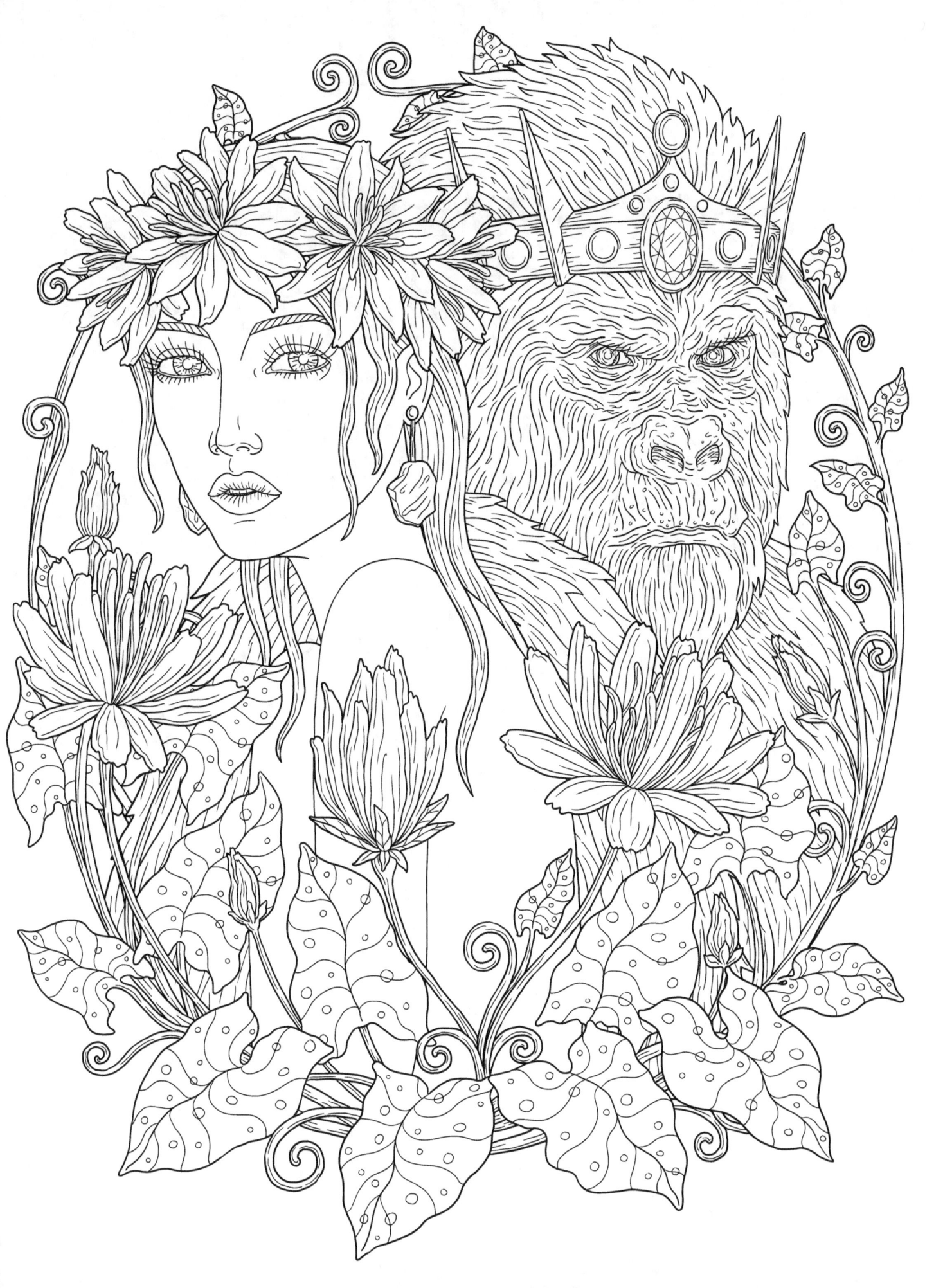

FLOWER SHOWER

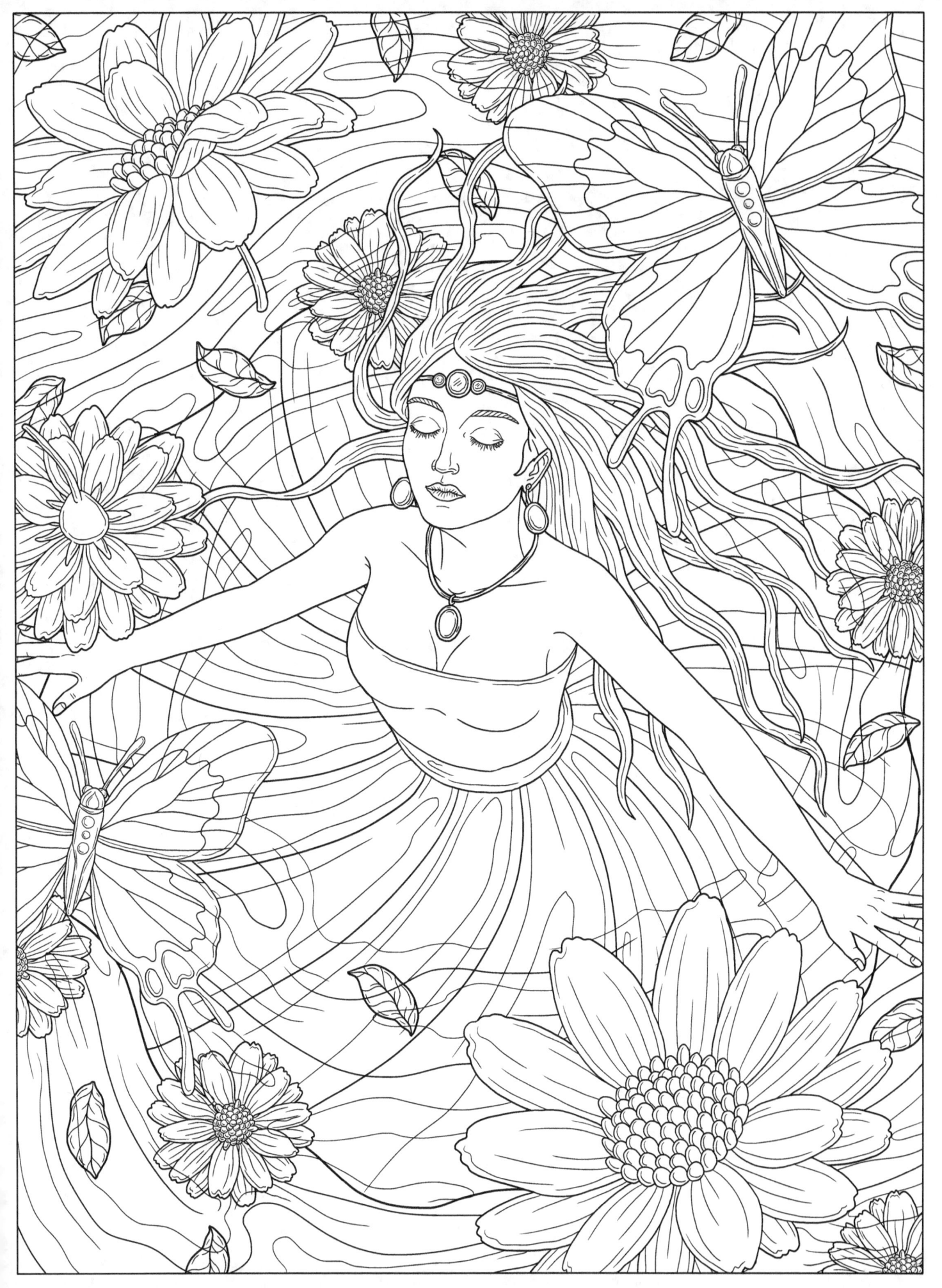

Equus Majestic

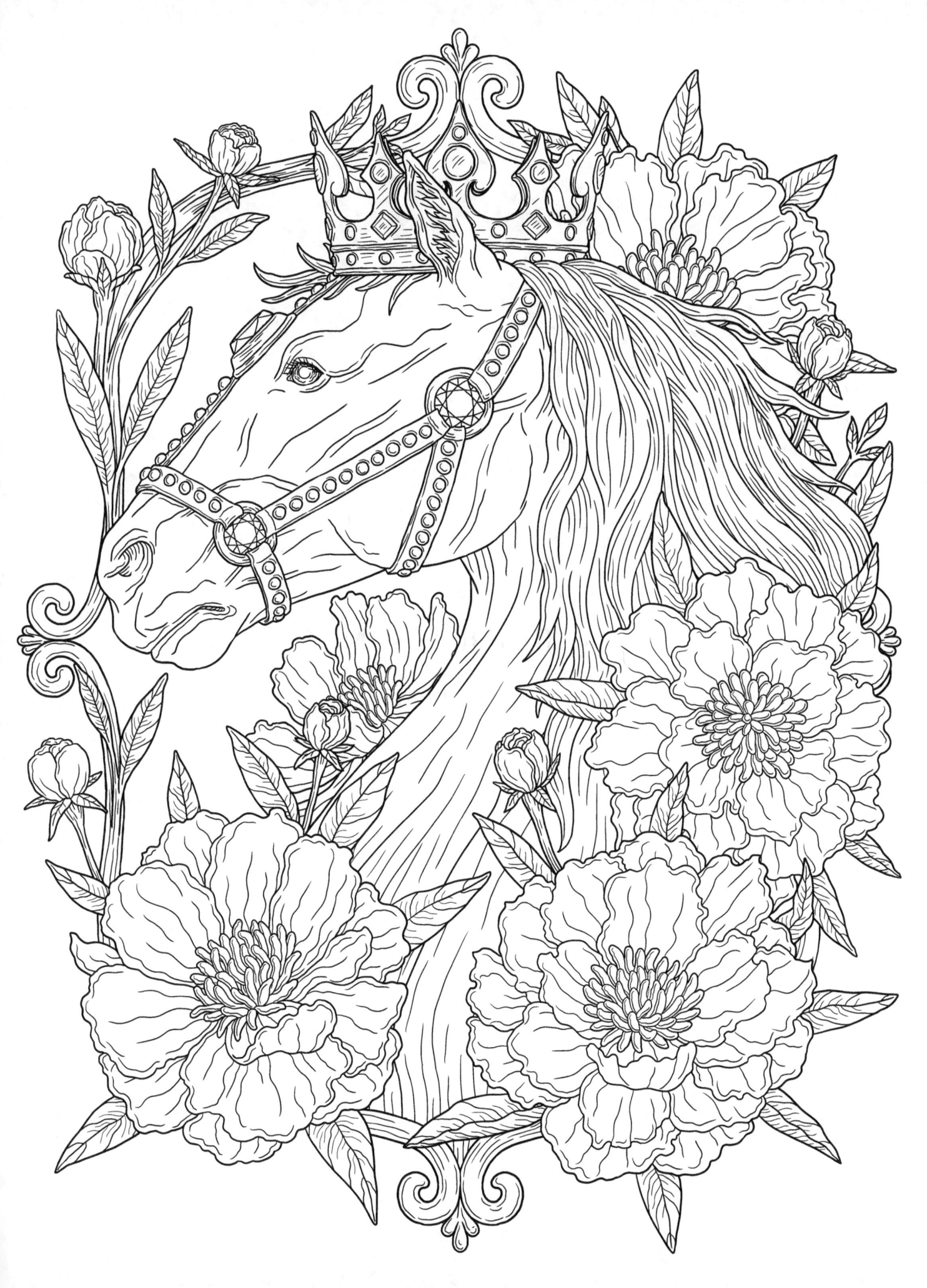

WARRIOR CYGNUS

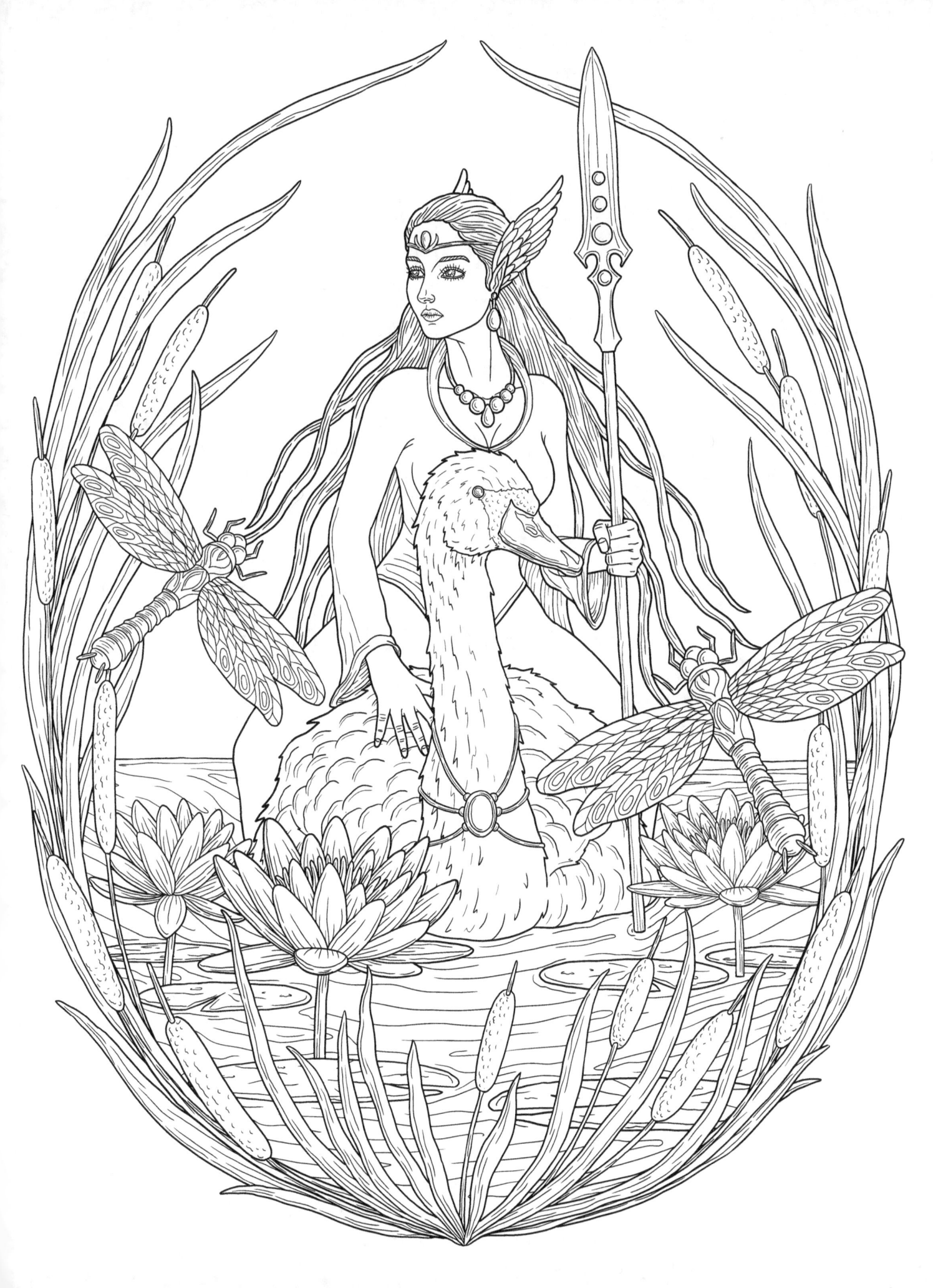

EMPRESS CORONATA

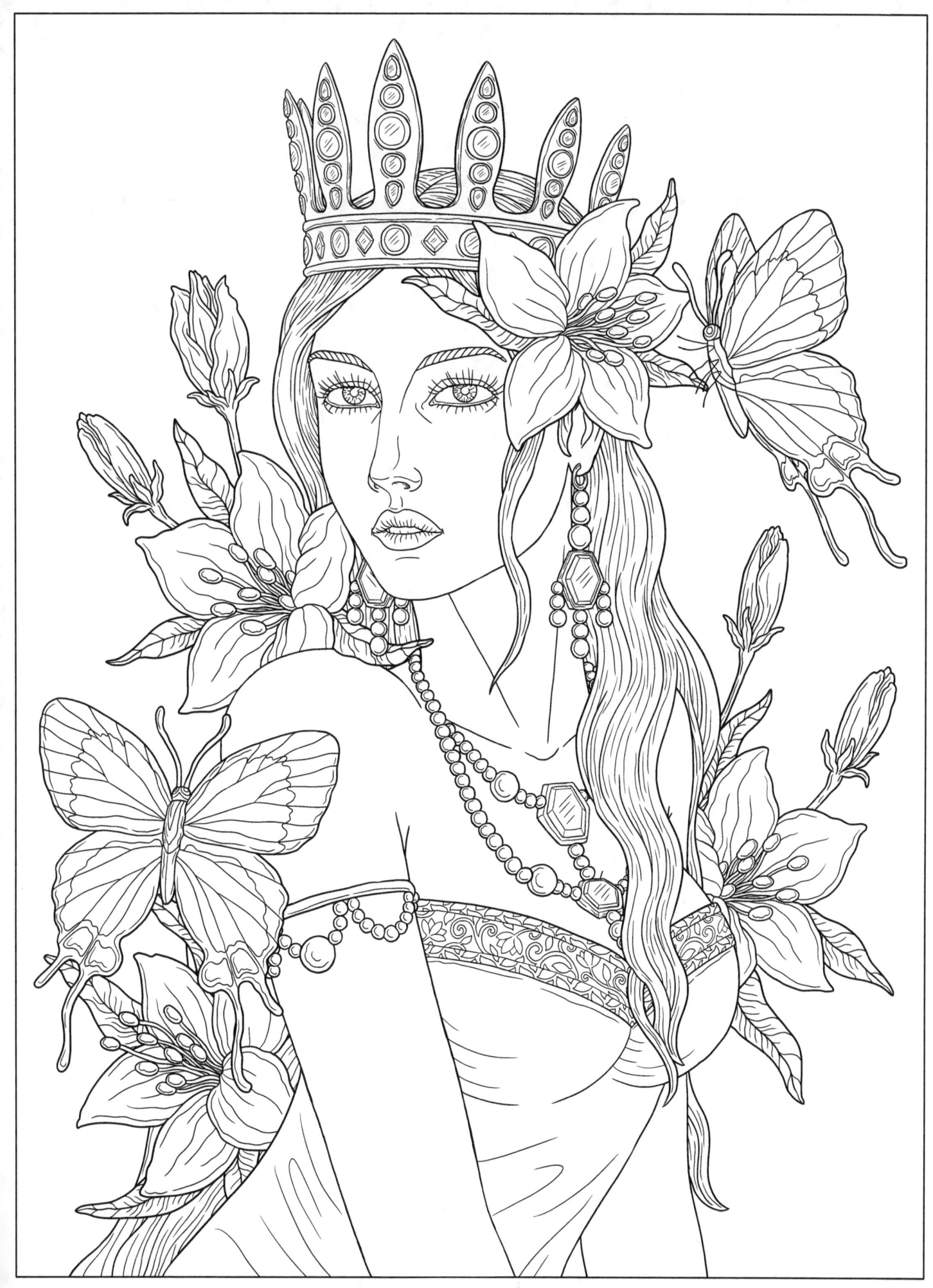

ALSO AVAILABLE
FROM VIVID PUBLISHERS

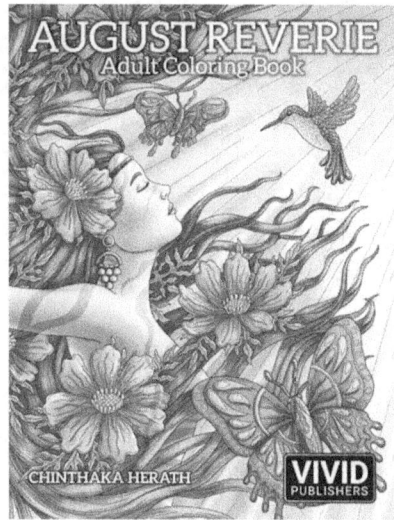
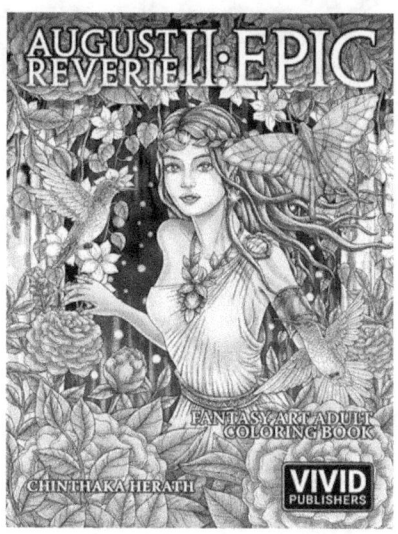
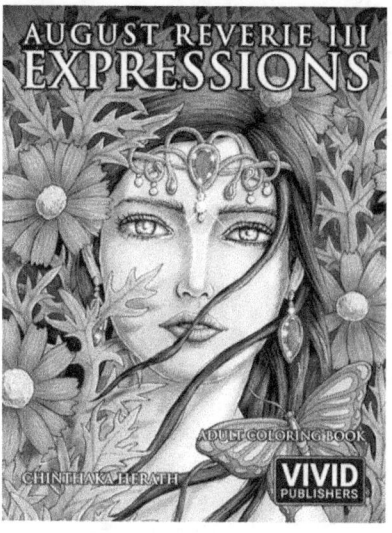
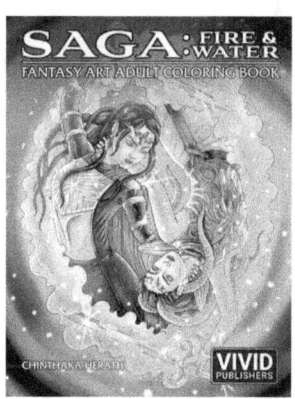
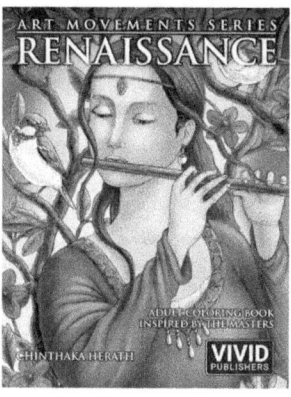
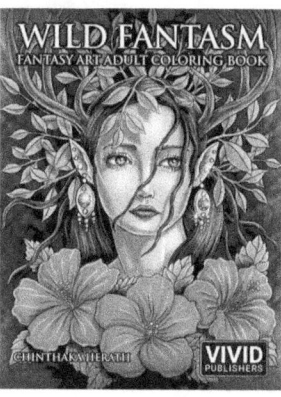
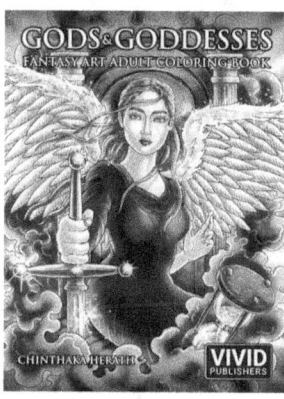

SUPPORT YOUR ARTIST CHINTHAKA HERATH AND GET EXCLUSIVE COLORING PAGES!

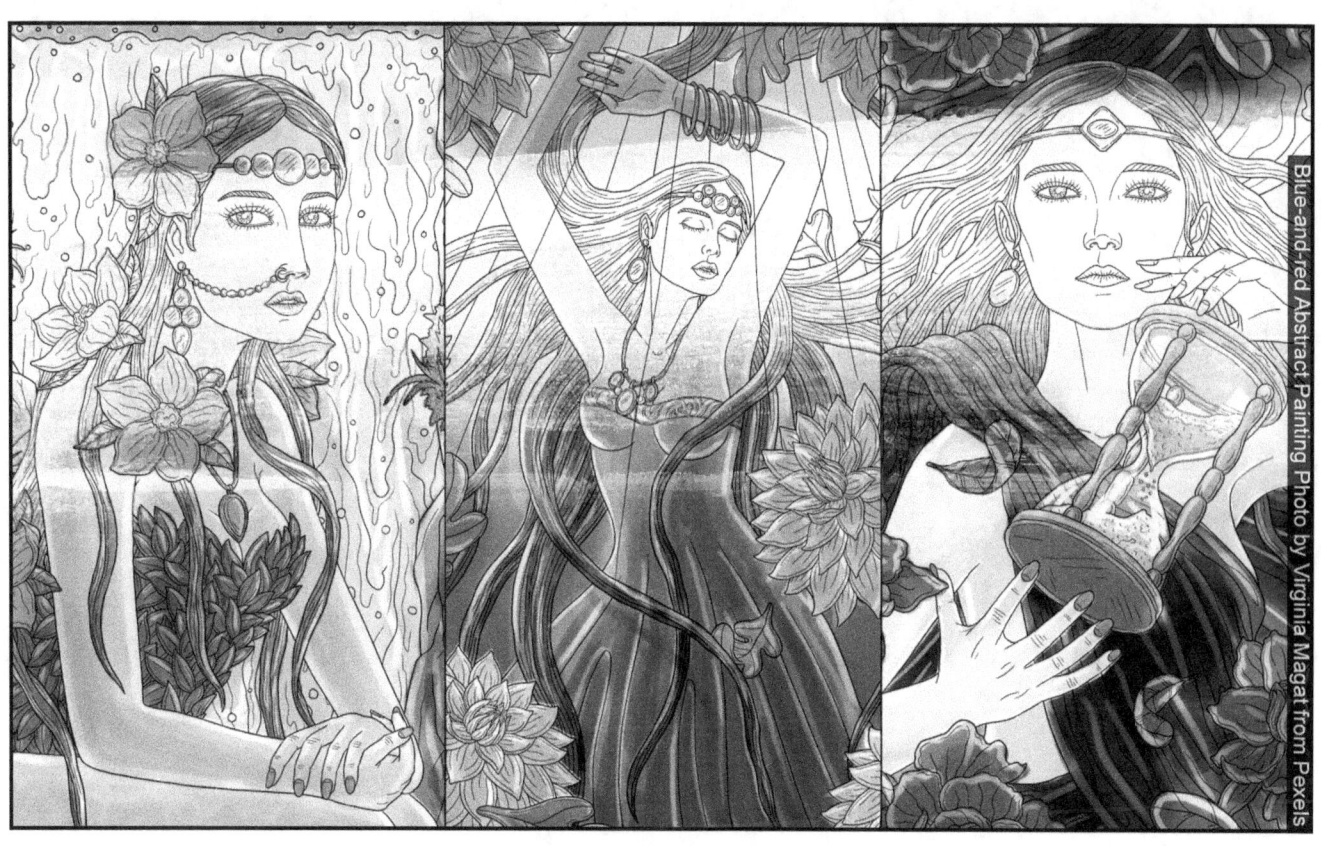

Blue-and-red Abstract Painting Photo by Virginia Magat from Pexels

Shown here are the pages available only for the month of February 2021.
New set of pages will be released every month.